MAKING PRESENTS

Clare Rosen
Illustrated by Lily Whitlock

CONTENTS

Series editor: Angela Wilkes

Hobby Horse

You will need:
a large old sock
scraps of material
or newspaper for
stuffing
a piece of felt
2 buttons
some wool
needle and thread
a ribbon
a broom handle

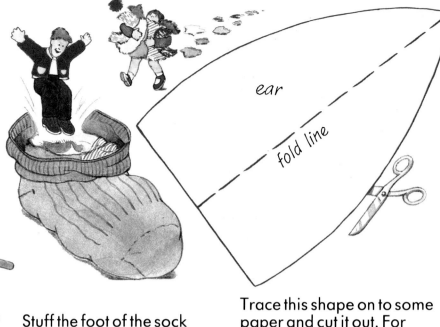

ear

fold line

Stuff the foot of the sock firmly with scraps of material or newspaper.

Trace this shape on to some paper and cut it out. For each ear, pin the shape on to felt and cut round it.

Fold the ears down the middle. Pin them to the sock and sew them on, using back stitch. (See page 25)

Sew on buttons for eyes. Sew a mouth in backstitch. Sew a line of wool loops down the neck for a mane.

Push the broom handle into the sock as far as the heel. Pack stuffing around it. Tie a ribbon round it to hold it on.

Pasta Necklace

Choose pasta shapes with a hole in the middle so that you can thread them. Paint them bright colours, using thick poster paint.

When the pasta shapes are dry, paint them with a coat of varnish. Wait for them to dry. Thread the shapes on to a ribbon and tie it in a bow.

To make beads hang down, thread the ribbon through two shapes, then back through the first.

3

Calendar Pictures

You will need :
a piece of card
glue & sticky tape
paints or things to
make a collage with
a calendar booklet
a piece of string

A calendar is easy to make and a good present for anyone at the beginning of the year. You could paint a picture or make a collage out of scraps of paper or odds and ends.

You can make a collage out of beans, rice, lentils or pasta. First draw a picture on a piece of card.

Pressed Flower Picture Calendar

You will need :
a piece of card
flowers and/or leaves
blotting paper
large books
glue and sticky tape
a calendar booklet
a piece of string

To make a picture from pressed flowers and leaves, you must collect them a few weeks in advance.

Carefully lay the flowers and leaves you have picked on to a sheet of blotting paper. Put another piece of blotting paper over them and put them inside a large book.

4

Spread glue on to part of the picture and press one sort of bean on to it. Glue different beans to each part of the picture.

When the glue is dry, gently shake off any loose bits. Tape a short string to the back, like this.

Glue a calendar booklet on to the bottom of the picture.

DECEMBER

BE CAREFUL WITH YOUR PRESSED FLOWERS—THEY ARE VERY FRAGILE

Close the book and stack heavy books on top. Leave them for at least two weeks.

Arrange your flowers and leaves on the card, then stick them on using only a tiny spot of glue.

JULY

5

Sweets

For about 20 truffles
you will need:

75g (3oz) cream cheese
1 teaspoon milk
100g (4oz) icing sugar
100g (4oz) drinking
    chocolate powder
vermicelli (chocolate
sprinkles) and drinking
chocolate powder for
    decoration

Truffles

Mix together the cheese and milk. Stir in the icing sugar and chocolate powder. Roll the mixture

into marble-sized balls in chocolate powder or vermicelli. Put them in the fridge for an hour to harden.

100g (4oz) ground
    almonds
75g (3oz) icing sugar
75g (3oz) sugar
1 beaten egg
1 teaspoon lemon juice
walnut halves and
    blanched almonds
dates   red and
        green food
        colouring

Making Marzipan

Mix together the icing sugar, ground almonds, sugar and lemon. Add enough beaten egg to make a stiff paste.

Divide the mixture into three balls. Add a drop of food colouring to two of the balls and knead it in.

Marzinuts

Window Sweets

Roll some of each colour marzipan into small balls. Press a nut on to the top of each ball.

Cut four pieces of marzipan, at least one from each colour, and roll them into long sausages. Push the rolls firmly together, two on top of the other two, and flatten them on all sides. Slice them into small squares.

Stuffed Dates

Cut open the dates and take out the stones. Fill them with marzipan. Then sprinkle them with sugar.

Put the sweets in a box or basket lined with pretty paper. Or use an empty jar with the label soaked off.

7

Humpty Dumpty Egg Cosy

You will need :
pink, yellow, blue
and green felt
red & yellow wool
a large needle
pins
scissors
a felt pen
a ruler
glue that will
stick fabric

Cut out a square of paper, each side 8cm long. (See p.25.) Fold it in half. Measure 4cm from the top corner. Draw a curved line across the corner, where the dotted line is. Cut along the line. Open the paper out.

Fold the yellow felt in half and pin the paper to it. Cut round it. Do the same with the pink felt.

Draw these shapes on different coloured bits of felt, using a felt pen, and cut them out. To make the collar, cut out a piece of felt 8cm by 3cm. Fold it in half and cut out a shape for the bow tie, like this.

Glue the collar, eyes and nose on to one piece of yellow felt. Sew a mouth with wool, using backstitch.*

Turn the felt over. Glue the hands and legs on to the back, as shown. Glue on strips of red wool for hair.

Glue a pink felt shape on to the back of the yellow piece. Glue the other yellow piece to the other pink one.

Put the two halves together with the pink felt on the inside. Sew them together round the curved edge using blanket stitch.*

Make an egg cosy in a different colour for each person.

*See page 25.

9

Kaleidoscope

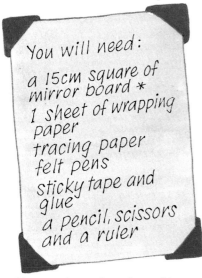

You will need:

a 15cm square of
mirror board *
1 sheet of wrapping
paper
tracing paper
felt pens
sticky tape and
glue
a pencil, scissors
and a ruler

*You can buy mirror board in art
and craft shops.

On the plain side of the mirror board, measure 5cm along
one edge and make a pencil mark. Measure another 5cm
along the edge and make another mark. Do the same on
the opposite edge and draw between the marks, like this.

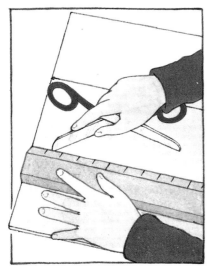

Score along the lines using
a ruler and the tip of the
scissors, like this. Do not cut
right through the card.

Fold the board along the
lines, so the mirror is inside.
Stick the edges together
with tape.

Stand the tube on the
tracing paper and trace
round the end. Do the same
on the wrapping paper. Cut
out the triangles of paper.

Carefully stick the triangle of tracing paper over one end of the tube with sticky tape.

Colour pieces of tracing paper with felt pens. Cut them into little bits and drop them into the tube.

Stick the wrapping paper triangle over the open end of the tube and make a hole in the middle with a pencil.

Cut out a piece of wrapping paper 17cm long and 15cm wide. Lay the tube down on it a little way from the edge. Glue the paper neatly all round the tube to cover it.

Hold the tube up to the light and look through the hole. Shake the kaleidoscope to make the patterns change.

Poppies and Daffodils

crepe paper
25 cm lengths of
garden wire for stems
black paper
strong glue
with a nozzle
scissors

poppies

Flower Centre

Cut out a piece of black paper about this size. Make cuts all along it, as shown.

Spread glue along it and wind it round the end of a wire stem.

Petals

Cut eight petals like this out of crêpe paper. Cut them so the grain (the crinkles) are running up and down.

grain

Shape the petals by stretching them a bit with your thumbs, like this. Then glue them round the centre.

Glue a long strip of green crêpe paper to the bottom of the flower. Wind it down the wire and glue the end down.

12

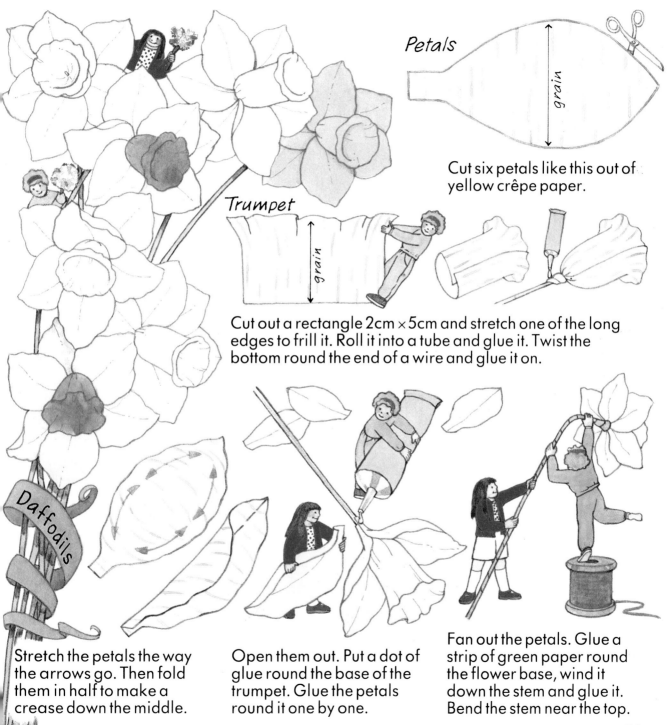

Petals

Cut six petals like this out of yellow crêpe paper.

Trumpet

grain

Cut out a rectangle 2cm × 5cm and stretch one of the long edges to frill it. Roll it into a tube and glue it. Twist the bottom round the end of a wire and glue it on.

Daffodils

Stretch the petals the way the arrows go. Then fold them in half to make a crease down the middle.

Open them out. Put a dot of glue round the base of the trumpet. Glue the petals round it one by one.

Fan out the petals. Glue a strip of green paper round the flower base, wind it down the stem and glue it. Bend the stem near the top.

13

Painted Eggs

Make a hole in the small end of each egg with a big needle. Make a bigger hole in the other end of the egg.

Blow hard into the small hole until all the egg comes out. Catch it in a bowl and keep it for cooking.

Wash the egg and dry it carefully.

Sit an egg on an egg cup and paint it. Paint one end, leave it to dry and then paint the other end.

If you are using more than one colour, paint the lighter colours first. Try different patterns and pictures.

When the egg is completely dry paint it with varnish.

14

Egg Mobile

Lay two stakes across each other and tie them together in the middle. Leave one end of the string long.

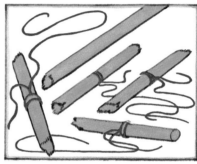

Break four short bits off the third stake. Tie a long piece of cotton to each one.

Push a bit of stake right into the bigger hole of each egg. Do not let go of the cotton.

ONCE INSIDE, THE STAKE CANNOT GET OUT

Tie the eggs on to the stakes like this, and cut off any long spare cotton.

Ask a friend to hold the string for you. Move the eggs along the stakes until the mobile balances well.

15

Party Hats

Sun Hat 55 cm square of card crepe paper tissue paper pencil, string, scissors and sticky tape

Wizard's Hat
50cm square of black or dark blue card
silver foil
scissors
glue and sticky tape

War Bonnet
corrugated cardboard 50cm long & 5cm wide
tissue paper
straws
scissors, glue and sticky tape
paints or felt tips

Wizard's Hat

Cut out a piece of card 50cm square.* Fold it into a cone and stick it down with tape.

Trim the bottom edge with scissors to make it straight.

Cut star and moon shapes out of silver foil and stick them on to the hat with glue.

16   *See page 25.

Sun Hat

Draw a circle with a 25cm radius on card.* Cut it out. Cut two slits opposite each other, 8cm from the centre.

Cut a ribbon of crêpe paper about 10cm wide and 1 metre long. Fold it in half lengthways and thread it through the slits. Make some paper flowers (see page 12) and stick them on to the hat with tape.

War Bonnet

Cut out a piece of corrugated cardboard 50cm long and 5cm wide.

Paint a pattern on it. When the paint is dry, stick the ends together with tape.

Cut feather shapes out of tissue paper. Make them a bit shorter than the straws.

Glue the feathers on to the straws. Leave about 5cm of straw at the bottom.

Make cuts all along the feathers, as shown.

Push the ends of the straws into the holes in the corrugated cardboard.

17

Desk Tidy

You will need :
3 cardboard tubes
(from kitchen or
lavatory paper rolls)
2 sheets of wrapping
paper
a piece of card about
20cm × 15cm
4 empty matchboxes
scissors and glue
4 paper fasteners

This is a good present for a grown-up. It holds all sorts of useful things like pens, pencils and stamps.

Penholder

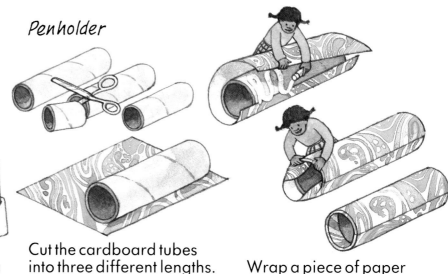

Cut the cardboard tubes into three different lengths. Cut out pieces of wrapping paper big enough to round each, with a little over.

Wrap a piece of paper round each tube. Glue the edges together and fold in the overlap at each end.

Base

Lay the piece of card on some wrapping paper. Draw round it and cut out the paper. Glue it on to the card to make the base.

Stamp Box

NEVER PLAY WITH MATCHES

Take the drawers out of the matchboxes. Cut 4 strips of paper the same width and twice as long as the drawers. Wrap them round the drawers and glue them on.

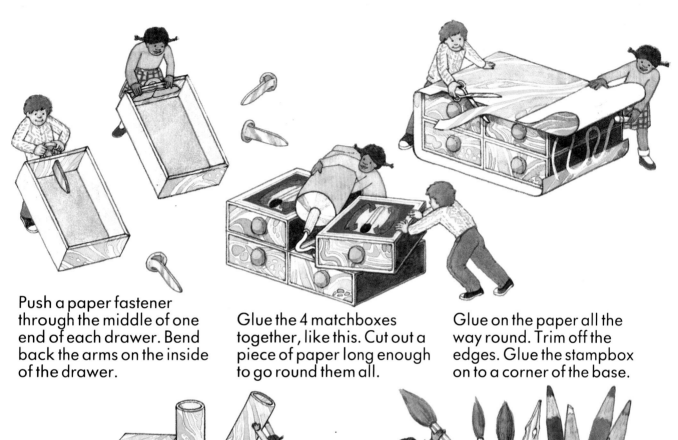

Push a paper fastener through the middle of one end of each drawer. Bend back the arms on the inside of the drawer.

Glue the 4 matchboxes together, like this. Cut out a piece of paper long enough to go round them all.

Glue on the paper all the way round. Trim off the edges. Glue the stampbox on to a corner of the base.

Put glue round one end of each tube and stick them on to the base. Glue them together where they touch.

Piggy Bank

You make this pig out of 'papier-mâché', which means mashed paper. It takes a bit of time to make.

Tear about four pages of newspaper into small bits. Put them in a bowl of water to soak for a few minutes.

Press a layer of paper round the orange. Put paste all over it, then another layer of paper. Do this until there are six layers of paper.

Put the orange somewhere warm overnight. When the paper is dry cut it all round the orange. Take out the orange. Cut a slot as big as a large coin along the edge of one half. Glue the halves back together again.

Cover the ball with two more layers of paper. Use the edges of the newspaper so the ball ends up white.

20

Glue four toothpaste tube tops on to the bottom for legs. Cut the end off a cork with a knife and glue it on for a nose.

Put another layer of glue and paper all over the piggy, covering the legs and nose.

Paint the pig with thick paint. When it is dry, paint on a face and a tail.

When the paint is dry, you can varnish it to make it shiny.

21

Printing Paper

Marbling

> ALWAYS PUT THE TOP BACK ON THE WHITE SPIRIT BOTTLE STRAIGHT AWAY

You will need:

FOR MARBLING
2 colours of oil paint *
white spirit
a big bowl, a plate & a knife

FOR POTATO PRINTS
a big potato
a knife and a plate
paints
paper

FOR STENCILS
thin card
paints and scissors
an old toothbrush
paper

Put blobs of the paint* on a plate. Mix a few drops of white spirit into it with a knife to make it runny.

Pour a little water into a bowl. The bowl must be at least as big as your paper.

Shake the paint from the knife on to the water and swirl it round.

Gently lay your paper on top of the water, then carefully lift it off again. Leave the paper to dry.

Clean the plate, knife and bowl with white spirit, then wash them in hot soapy water.

22   *You can buy small tubes of oil paint at art shops.

Potato Prints

Cut a big potato in half. Cut a shape on the flat side, then cut away the potato round it so the shape stands out.

Mix some paint with a little water on a plate. Press the cut side of the potato down into it.

Press the potato on to paper to make a print of the shape. Make more prints all over the paper to make a pattern.

Stencils

Draw a shape on a piece of thin card. Push the point of your scissors into it and cut it out to make a stencil.

Hold the stencil down firmly on a big piece of paper. Dip an old toothbrush into paint. Hold it over the stencil and stroke the bristles.

Spatter the paint evenly over the stencil shape. Lift off the stencil and do the same again until the pattern is all over the paper.

Wrapping Presents

MAKE YOUR PRESENTS LOOK AS PRETTY AS POSSIBLE. WRAP COLOURED RIBBON OR TAPE ROUND THEM AND TIE IT IN BOWS

You will need:
wrapping paper
sticky tape
ribbon

Square present

IF THE PRESENT IS BREAKABLE OR A DIFFICULT SHAPE TO WRAP, PUT IT IN A BOX FIRST

Cut out a piece of wrapping paper big enough to go right round the present. Wrap it round the present and stick it with tape.

Fold down one end, then fold in the sides. Fold the bottom flap up and stick it down with tape. Do the same at the other end.

Round present

Lay the present on the paper. Cut out the paper so it has a 10cm overlap at each end.

Roll the paper round the present and stick it down with tape in the middle. Bunch up the ends and twist them a little to make the present look like a cracker.